NATIONAL GEOGRAPHIC
KIDS

COOL
ANIMALS
STICKER ACTIVITY
BOOK

Pull out the sticker sheets and keep
them by you when you complete each page.
There are also lots of extra stickers to
use in this book or anywhere you want!
Have fun!

**NATIONAL
GEOGRAPHIC**
Washington, D.C.

Picture credits: pp1–40: all images Shutterstock except for: **Fotolia:** 18 tm, 29 m; **Fotosearch:** 38 bl; **Make Believe Ideas:** 1 tl, 2 tl; bl, 3 tl, 4 mr; br, 5 br, 9 tl; m; bm, 11 br, 12 ml, 13 tm, 14 ml, 16 ml; mr, 17 br (olive leaf), 18 tl; br; bm, 21 mr (yellow/black frog), 22 mr, 23 tr; m; br; bm, 25 bl, 26 tl; tm; tr, 28 m, 30 bm; br, 32 mr; m; br, 33 tr; bm (beetle x2), 35 bl, 36 bl; bm; br, 37 br, 40 mr; bl; **Mark O'Shea:** 15 ml (gecko); **National Geographic Stock:** 2 br, 8 br, 21 tr (American green tree frog), 24 tr, 33 mr, 36 ml, 40 tm.

Sticker pages: all images Shutterstock except for: **Fotolia:** 28,29 silver fish bl; **Fotosearch:** 4,5 purple jellyfish; turtle, 10,11 purple jellyfish, 38,39 stingray; purple jellyfish; **Make Believe Ideas:** 2,3 frog; olive leaf; tortoise; yellow butterfly; parrot; daisy; tiger face; owl; blue butterfly, 4,5 one spot foxface; golden butterfly fish; starfish; black/yellow fish small; queen angelfish; spiral shell; green fish; whelk shell; cockleshell, 6,7 sweets; football; cupcake, 8,9 zebra x2; mountain goat; butterfly x3; tortoise; lizard; tiger x2; lion x3; California kingsnake; rhino x2; giraffe x3; elephant; crocodile, 10,11 seahorse; cinnamon anemonefish; one spot foxface; blacktip reef shark; cockleshell; green fish; black/yellow fish small; golden butterfly fish; queen angelfish; whelk shell; starfish, 12,13 seagull, 14,15 spider m; beetles tl, m, bl, br, mr, tr; leaf insect x2; olive leaf, 16,17 spiders ml, bm, tr; fly hl, mr, 20,21 frogs tl, tm, tr, bm, 22,23 baboon and young; train; ice cream; donut ducky leaf monkey; sunglasses; monkey toy; car; glbbon; spoon; toothbrush, 24,25 lion x2; tiger x3; black leopard br; jaguar, 28,29 green fish; sardine, 30,31 giraffe tm, tr, m; flamingo, 32,33 spade; marbles; snake; burrowing scorpion; hat, 34,35 sandwich; gingerbread; boat; rose; watch; scissors, 36,37 polar bear x2; snowy owl; sealions; fur seal; reindeer, 38,39 cockleshell; crab; starfish; one spot foxface; golden butterfly fish; yellow/black fish small; seahorse; whelk shell; spiral shell; queen angelfish; green fish, 40 parrot; bat; red-eyed tree frog x2; tiger x2; milksnake; red leaf x3; rockhopper penguin; rabbit x2; zebra; mountain goat; olive leaf; lion x2; northern saw-whet owl; elephant; rhino x2; emerald tree boa; hamadryas baboon; California kingsnake; giraffe x2; iguana; kitten; polar bear; beetles tl, tm, tr, ml, m, mr, bl, br; stag beetle x2; leaf insect; tarantula; moth; cockroach; **Mark O'Shea:** 14,15 tm (gecko); **National Geographic Stock:** 22,23 golden marmoset x2, 32,33 meerkat, 40 otter; **123RF:** 10,11 desjardini tang, 36,37 yellow tang, 38,39 Hawaiian squirrelfish; desjardini tang.

Spot the animals with stripes!
Help the tiger get through the forest maze!

START

Sticker the animals he finds on the way!

FINISH

Tigers are the biggest cats in the world!

Sticker one tiger's face and color the other!

Every tiger has a different pattern of stripes!

Color a tiger pattern!

Color and sticker more amazing animals with spots and stripes!

Sticker a hunting tiger!

What animal is this? Complete the word.

ze b r a

Sharks are amazing!

Sticker a blacktip reef shark!

lemon shark

zebra shark

clown fish

WARNING

Use the grid to draw a shark!

Draw here

4

Sticker a shark's tooth!

Sticker a hammerhead shark!

great white shark

Sharks have sharp teeth and powerful bodies.

Color the sea life and sticker more fish friends!

What else lives in the ocean?

5

These beastly **bugs** like to buzz, battle, leap . . . and hide!

BUZZ!

stag beetles

BATTLE!

LEAP!

grasshopper

HIDE!

leaf insect

Sticker a crazy pattern onto the ladybug!

Draw your own bug!

7

Elephants are **big** and **strong.**

START

Find your way through the elephant maze.

FINISH

OUCH! Let go!

Draw the other half of the elephant.

Elephants are the largest animals that live on land today.

Sticker animals at the water hole.

African elephants

hippo

Sticker this dangerous animal!

bongo

impala

What lives under the sea?

Finish the dot-to-dot, then add color!

Octopuses do not have skeletons!

hawksbill sea turtle

Color the animals and add stickers to complete the ocean scene.

Scary fish

Ugly

wolffish

Draw more teeth!

anglerfish

Scary and hairy

striated frogfish

blacktip reef shark

reef
squid

11

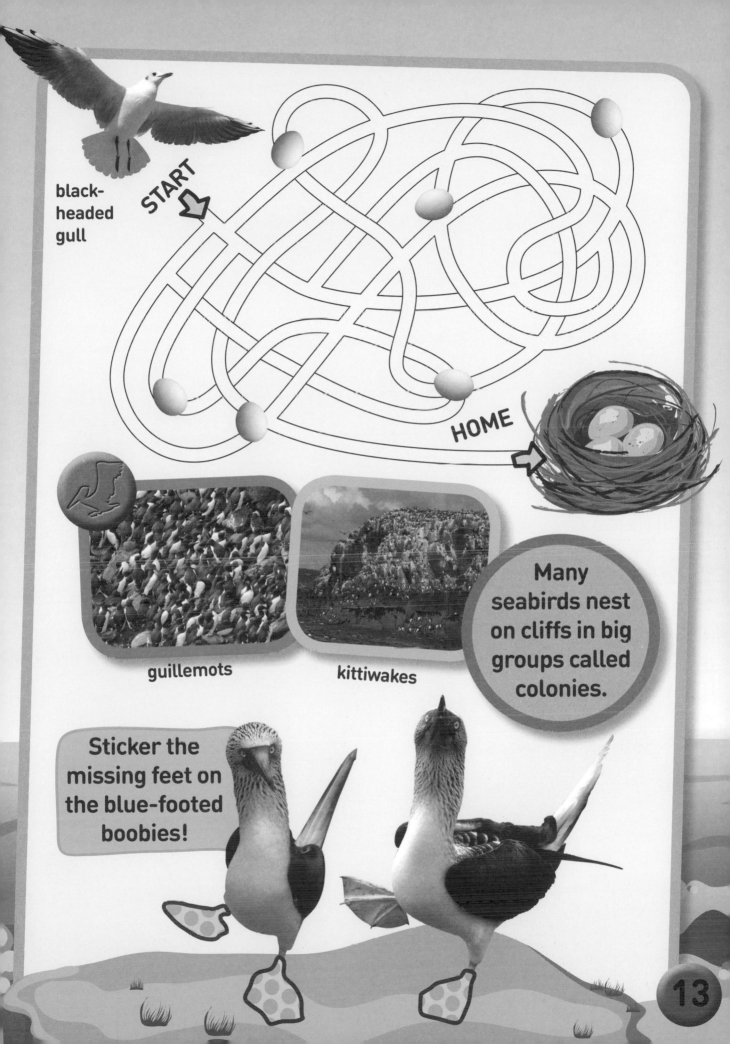

black-headed gull

START

HOME

guillemots

kittiwakes

Many seabirds nest on cliffs in big groups called colonies.

Sticker the missing feet on the blue-footed boobies!

Who's watching?

Lizards love to eat **bugs.**

YUM YUM

veiled chameleon

Madagascar day gecko

Draw the lizards' tongues.

leopard gecko

Sticker the yummy bugs!

green iguana

Sticker the colorful chameleons!

panther chameleon

panther chameleon

juvenile veiled chameleon

Sticker more leaves.

A gecko in danger can detach its tail to distract a predator and escape.

tokay gecko

frilled lizard

Some lizards have frills.

Some lizards have horns.

Sticker the missing horn, tail, and frill.

Jackson's chameleon

frilled lizard

15

Spiders have long legs!

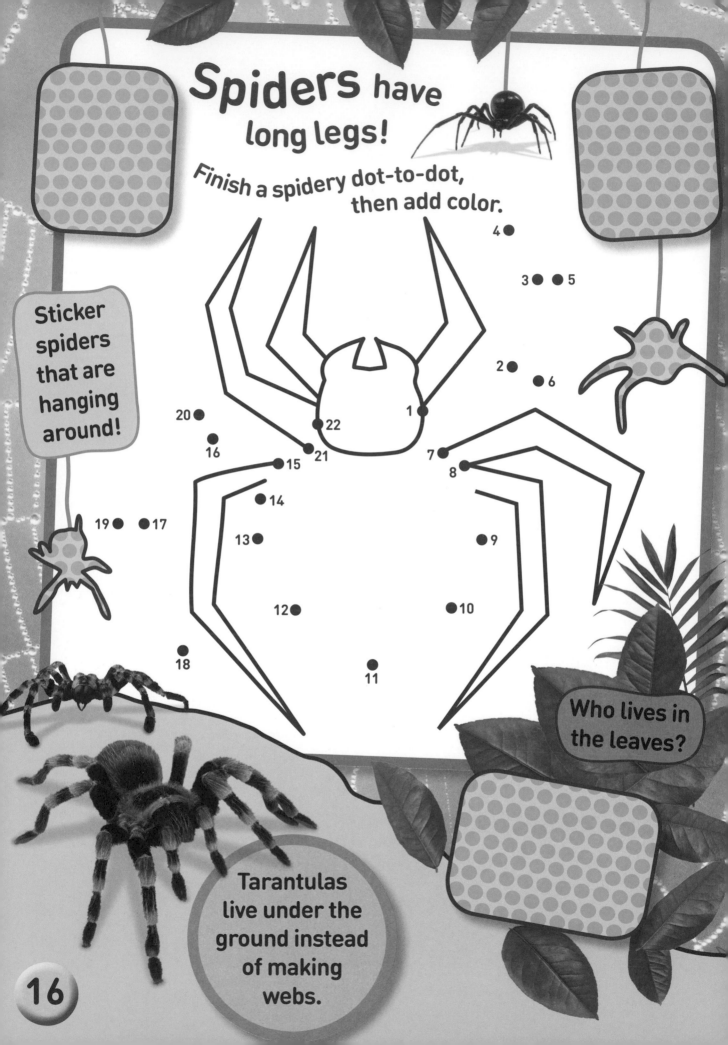

Finish a spidery dot-to-dot, then add color.

Sticker spiders that are hanging around!

Who lives in the leaves?

Tarantulas live under the ground instead of making webs.

4
3 ● ● 5
2 ● ● 6
1
22
21
20 ● ● 16
15
14
13 ●
19 ● ● 17
12 ●
18
7
8
9
10
11

Sticker flies for the spiders to eat.

orb weaver

Some spiders spin webs to catch food.

giant orb weaver

Most spiders have eight eyes.

jumping spider

Find who is hiding in the pots!

black widow

17

Wolves are great hunters!

Follow the lines to see who found the deer!

gray wolves

Sticker more wolf tracks!

Sticker the wolves coming out to play!

18

fallow deer

Use the grid to draw a wolf!

Draw here

Finish the dot-to-dot, then add color!

Wolves can find each other across long distances by howling.

Wolves live in groups called packs.

Sticker the missing howling wolves!

gray wolves

19

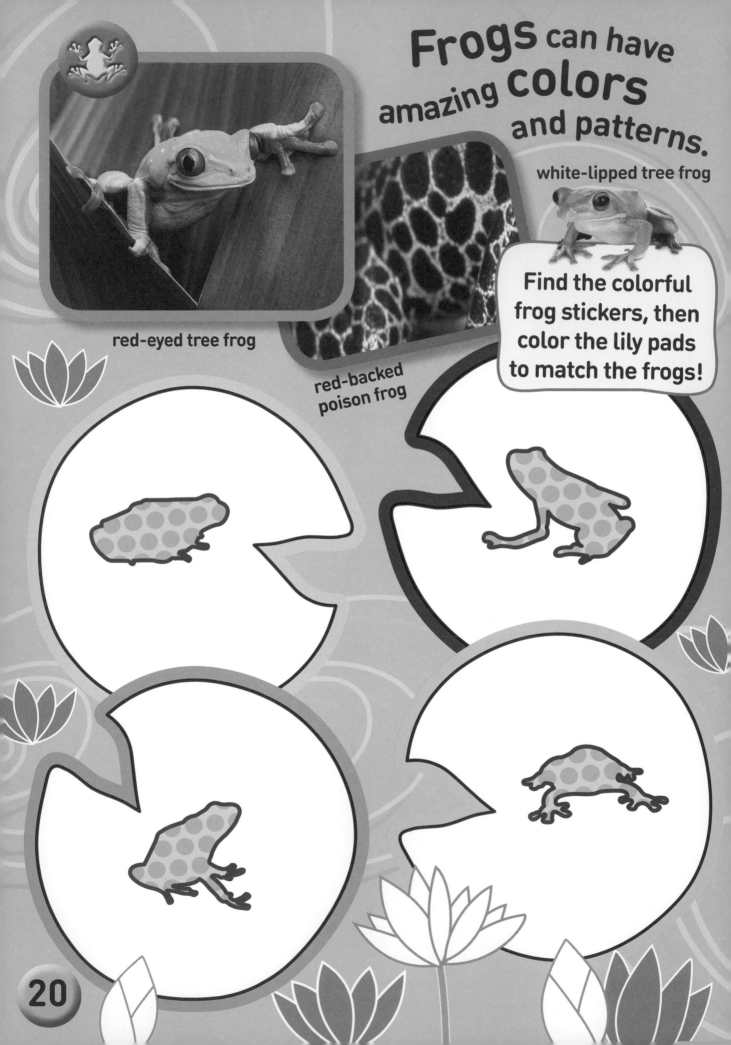

Frogs can have amazing colors and patterns.

red-eyed tree frog

red-backed poison frog

white-lipped tree frog

Find the colorful frog stickers, then color the lily pads to match the frogs!

20

Stickers for pages 2 and 3

Stickers for pages 4 and 5

Stickers for pages 6 and 7

Stickers for pages 8 and 9

Stickers for pages 10 and 11

Stickers for pages 12 and 13

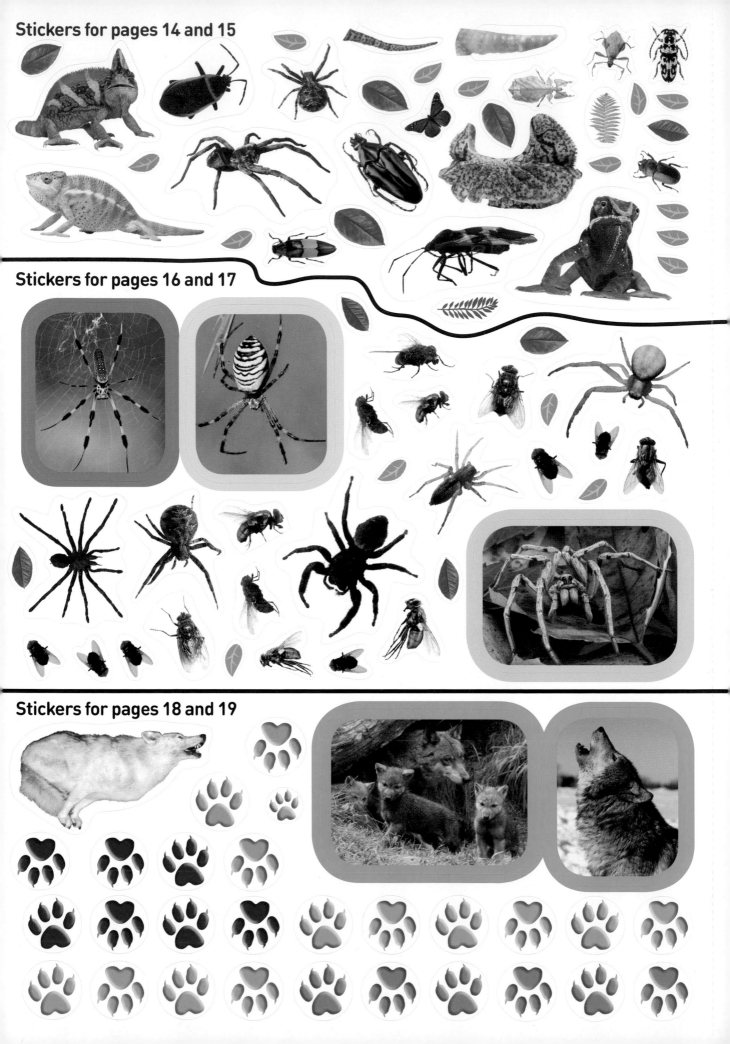

Stickers for pages 14 and 15

Stickers for pages 16 and 17

Stickers for pages 18 and 19

Stickers for pages 20 and 21

Stickers for pages 22 and 23

Stickers for pages 24 and 25

ROAR!

Stickers for pages 26 and 27

Stickers for pages 28 and 29

ROAR!

Stickers for pages 30 and 31

Stickers for pages 32 and 33

Stickers for pages 34 and 35

Stickers for pages 36 and 37

HOOT!

Stickers for pages 38 and 39

Stickers for page 40

Extra stickers

Sticker jumping frogs.

Some frogs can jump over 50 times their own body length!

African bullfrog

blue poison dart frog

black-and-yellow poison dart frog

American green tree frog

strawberry poison dart frog

How many frogs landed on the leaf?

Sticker spots onto the frog and add color.

Who's climbing?

It's a **primate** party!

What has the baboon stolen?

Most monkeys and apes like to sleep in a cozy nest built out of branches.

hamadryas baboon

Color this happy monkey!

CUTE!

SCARY!

Sticker more primates!

22

Sticker some banana snacks for the gorilla.

silverback gorilla

Draw a monkey face!

chimpanzee

23

Africa is home to **cool cats!**

What does the lion say?

Sticker lion cubs!

A lioness has no mane and looks after cubs.

Color the lion!

Draw and color tall grass to hide the lion!

blue-and-
yellow macaw

Sticker more wild cats!

cheetah

Burmese python

California kingsnake

milksnake

Snakes that hiss and rattle!

Snakes, like all reptiles, shed their skin to reveal a new layer.

Sticker a bright pattern onto the snake!

royal python

Find 5 snake eggs hidden on the page!

Who's hiding?

green tree python

Color the snakes and find the one that's different!

emerald tree boa

START

Wiggle your way through the snake maze!

Color the cobra!

king cobra

FINISH

27

Creatures with paws and claws!

What do bears shout?

Bears have big paws.

grizzly bear paw

Bears can catch fish as they swim upstream!

Sticker fish in the stream!

brown bear

28

SLEEPING!

Koalas aren't bears. They are actually related to kangaroos!

Sticker who is hiding in the eucalyptus leaves!

EATING!

CLIMBING!

START

FINISH

Help Mom find her baby!

Color the climbing koalas!

29

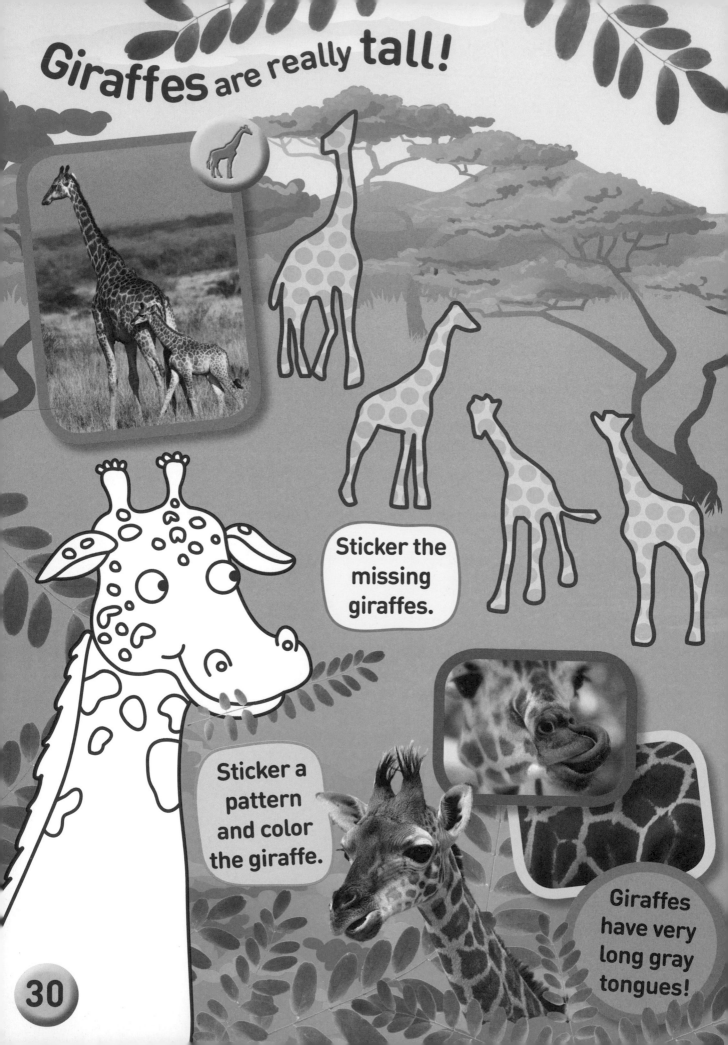

Draw, color, and sticker to make fun animal faces!

Add the stickers, then follow the lines to see who gets to the water.

Desert creatures beat the heat!

How many beetles do you see?

Taurus beetle

A scorpion has a stinger in its tail.

imperial scorpion

Sticker more scorpions!

rhinoceros beetle

Color the beetle!

ground beetle

burrowing scorpion

white-spotted assassin bug

figeater beetle

32

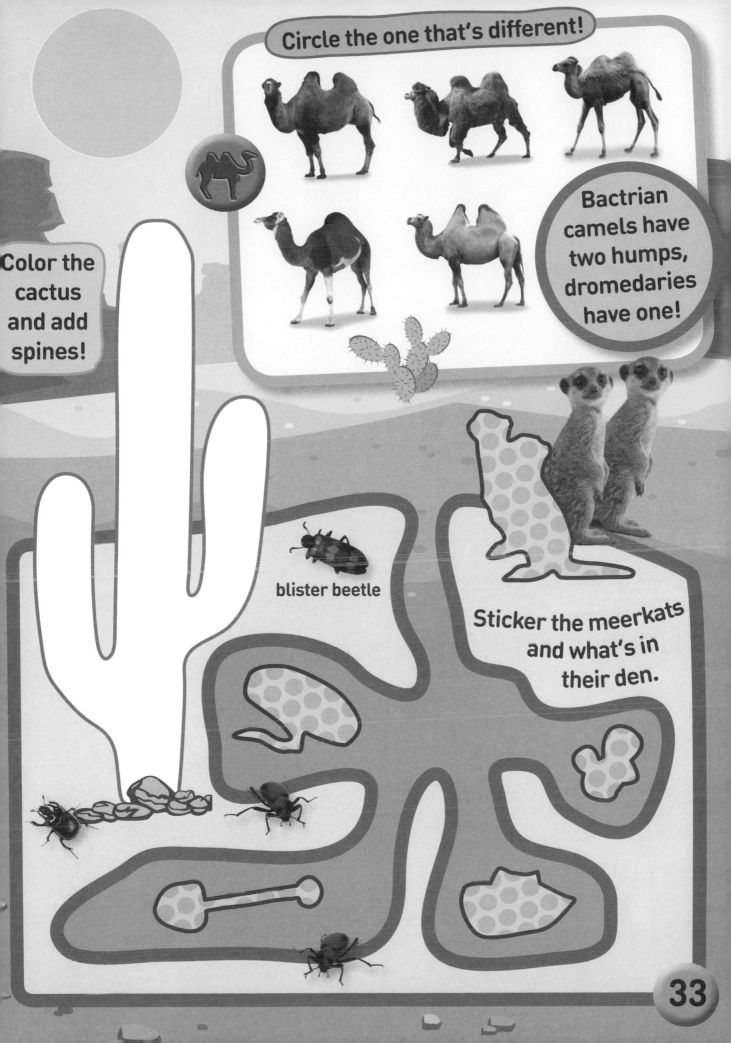

Circle the one that's different!

Bactrian camels have two humps, dromedaries have one!

Color the cactus and add spines!

blister beetle

Sticker the meerkats and what's in their den.

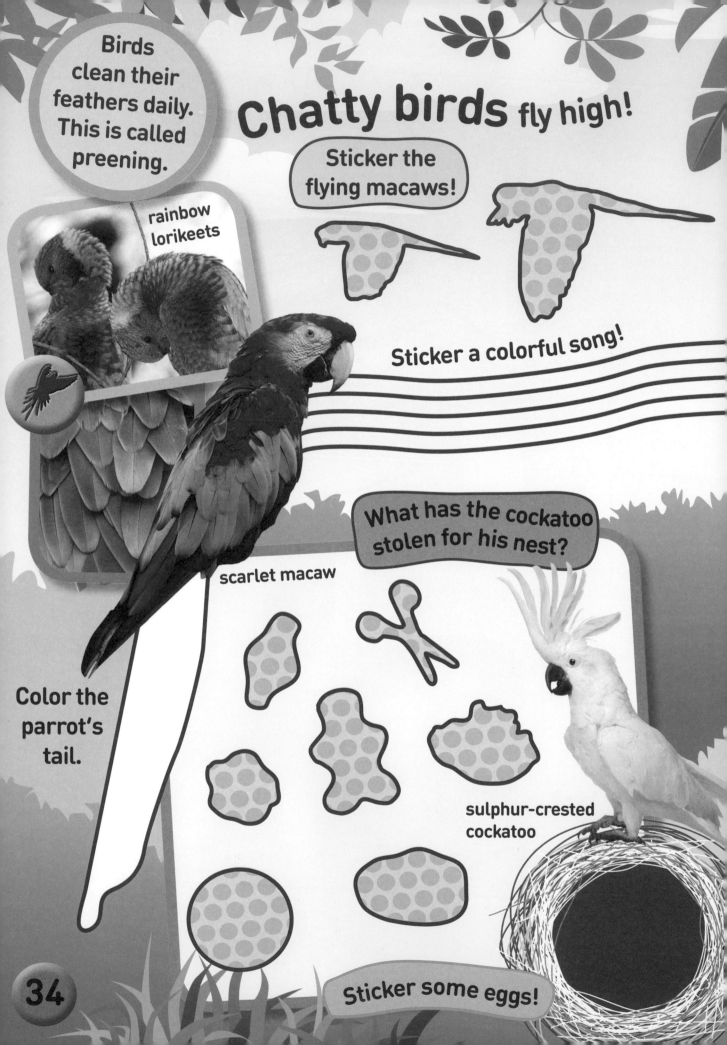

Animals have **icy adventures!**

Find a snowy owl!

Sticker more animals who live in the snow!

Arctic fox

Arctic hare

rockhopper penguin

Sticker animals playing by the icy water!

fur seal

Adélie penguin

36

Penguins cannot fly, but they swim very well!

Use the grid to finish drawing the penguin!

Follow the lines to see which penguin gets to the water!

king penguin

Sticker more snowflakes!

Color the penguin's bucket, then fill it with fish!

Adélie penguin

37

loggerhead
sea turtle

Turtles and rays
are awesome!

Sea turtles
can live up to
80 years!

Sticker the
missing sea
creatures!

Color the ray and
draw more spots!

blue-spotted
stingray

Sticker and color animals hiding in the seaweed!

Circle the fish that is different!

bannerfish

copperband butterfly fish

blue ring angelfish

clown fish

yellow boxfish

multibarred angelfish

39

Awesome animals!

red-eyed
tree frog

bottlenose dolphins

rainbow finch

orangutan

Who is stealing the eggs?

green iguana

A polar
bear has
black
skin!

Sticker the animals eating!

polar bear

Who is upside down?

Sticker and draw your favorite animals!